# Amazing Adventure and Survival Stories for Young and Curious

## Magda Lena

# Contents

# Get Your Free Quiz Book

https://do-you-want-to-know-more.my.canva.site/about

# Disclaimer

Greetings, dear reader! Before you embark on this splendid journey through the pages of " Amazing Adventure and Survival Stories for Young and Curious" we must lay down a few pebbles of wisdom:

**Fanciful Flights of Fancy:** The stories within are a delightful blend of reality and imagination, akin to finding a talking mouse in your cereal box – unexpected but thoroughly entertaining. While inspired by the world's wonders and the human spirit's bravado, these tales are primarily fictional. Any resemblance to actual events, locales, or persons, living or extinct (like a dodo), is purely coincidental and not intended.

**Educational, But Not a Textbook**: While we aim to sprinkle bits of knowledge and wisdom throughout these tales, like chocolate chips in a cookie, please remember this book is not a substitute for educational textbooks or survival guides. For learning how to tie an actual knot or identify a real bear in the woods, do turn to professional guides and educators.

**Adventure with Care:** Our tales of adventure and derring-do are meant to inspire and amuse, not to serve as blueprints for backyard escapades or wilderness exploration. We encourage all young explorers to undertake adventures responsibly and under the guidance of a responsible adult, preferably one who knows how to pitch a tent without invoking a rain dance.

**Diversity of Characters:** Our cast of characters, from brave boys to gallant girls and whimsical wildlife, is as varied as the flavors in a candy shop. We celebrate diversity and inclusion, and any portrayal is aimed at sharing joy and wonder, never to offend or stereotype.

**Bedtime Usage:** These stories are perfect for bedtime and are designed to transport dreamers to lands of adventure and intrigue. However, we hold no liability for any cases of "Just one more story, please!" that might lead to late-night reading marathons.

**Health and Safety:** Remember, exploring the great outdoors or even the corridors of one's imagination should always be done with care for one's health and safety. Please don't climb out of windows to meet giants or attempt to fly using umbrellas.

**Enjoyment Guaranteed:** We sincerely hope this book brings you joy, laughter, and perhaps a touch of the marvelous. Our mission is accomplished if you are smiling, chuckling, or daydreaming of grand adventures.

So, buckle up your imaginary seatbelt, open the pages, and dive into the magical world waiting inside. Happy reading!

# CHAPTER 1

# Lost in the Whispering Woods: The Mystery of the Moss-Covered Map - Navigating the forest with ancient secrets.

ONCE UPON A TIME, in a village where the houses had roofs as pointy as wizard hats, there lived a curious girl named Eliza. Eliza had eyes as bright as the stars and a thirst for adventure as vast as the sea. One fine morning, with the sun playing peekaboo behind the clouds, Eliza decided to explore the Whispering Woods, which bordered the village like a giant green wall.

As she stepped into the woods, the trees seemed to lean in, whispering secrets of ancient times. Eliza, with her heart thumping like a drum at a festival, ventured deeper, guided by the chirping of birds and the rustling of leaves.

Suddenly, she stumbled upon something half-buried under a moss carpet– an old, tattered map. As Eliza discovered, the map was a puzzle, with cryptic symbols and winding paths leading to a mysterious 'X.' Her adventurous heart leaped! "A treasure in the Whispering Woods!" she exclaimed. The woods echoed her excitement with a gentle rustle.

With the map as her guide, Eliza journeyed through the woods. She learned to read the map by matching its landmarks – a crooked tree resembling an older man, a stream that giggled over pebbles, and a rock shaped like a sleeping bear.

As the day wore on, Eliza realized she was lost. The familiar path home was nowhere to be seen. A tinge of fear crept into her heart. The Whispering Woods, once friendly, now seemed vast and unknown. But Eliza remembered what her grandmother used to say, "In times of trouble, calm is your best friend."

Taking a deep breath, Eliza sat down and thought. She remembered the skills her father had taught her – to look for the North Star at night and how moss often grew on the northern side of trees. Using these clues, she oriented herself and the map.

Nightfall brought a velvet sky dotted with stars. Guided by the twinkling North Star, Eliza began her journey back. She marked her path by tying bits of her handkerchief to branches, ensuring she wouldn't go in circles.

The night was alive with sounds – an orchestra of crickets, the soft hooting of an owl, and the trees whispering. Although scared, Eliza felt a connection with nature she had never touched. She realized the woods were not just speaking to her but guiding her.

After hours, Eliza saw a light in the distance – the lanterns from her village! Bursting with relief and joy, she ran towards the light. As she emerged from the woods, the villagers, who had been searching for her, greeted her with cheers and hugs.

Eliza told them about the map and her adventure. The villagers listened, wide-eyed, as she recounted how she used the stars and the moss to find her way back. The old village storyteller, with a beard as long as a winter night, declared, "Eliza has not just found her way home, but also the treasure of the Whispering Woods – the wisdom to navigate the unknown."

From that day on, Eliza was known as the Wise, and the Whispering Woods seemed less mysterious. Children would gather around her, eyes sparkling with curiosity, as she shared her tale and the lessons she learned:

1. Stay calm in the face of fear.

2. Nature is a guide if you know how
   to read it.

3. Adventure is lovely, but coming
   home is even better.

And as for the treasure marked on the
map? Well, that remained a mystery, perhaps
an adventure for another day. But for Eliza, the real treasure was the journey and
the wisdom she gained – far more valuable than gold or jewels.

# CHAPTER 2

# Stranded on the Secret Island: Coconuts and Castaways-Ingenious Island survival and unexpected friendships.

IN A WORLD NOT too different from ours, there was a boy named Max. Max had hair as unruly as a sea storm and a spirit that couldn't be tamed. His parents often said he was born with saltwater in his veins and a compass in his heart.

Max joined his parents on a sailing trip across the vast blue ocean one summer. The sea was like a giant, glittering sapphire, stretching as far as the eye could see. One fateful afternoon, as playful dolphins danced alongside their boat, a fierce storm appeared as if conjured by an angry sea wizard. The ship was tossed about like a toy, and Max was separated from his parents amidst the roaring storm.

He awoke on the sandy shore of an unknown island, with only the sea's gentle whisper for company. Max's heart sank like a heavy anchor. But he remembered his father's words, "In the heart of the storm, be the calm." Gathering his courage, Max stood up to face his new reality.

The island was a paradise lost – a jungle teeming with life, bordered by a beach where palm trees swayed like dancers. Max's first task was to find fresh water.

Recalling his survival shows, he searched for a stream, knowing that stagnant water was a no-go. Luck smiled on him as he saw a fresh, bubbling brook.

Next, Max needed food. The island was generous – there were coconuts, which he learned to open by smashing them against sharp rocks. He also found edible berries but remembered his mother's caution: "Not all berries are friends; some are foes." So, he tested them for safety, crushing a bit against his wrist to see if it caused a reaction.

Shelter was his next priority. Max built a small hut by the beach using palm leaves and branches. It wasn't a palace, but it was home. As nights fell, the island transformed. The sky became a canvas of stars, and the jungle a symphony of unknown sounds. Max felt fear creeping in, but he held onto the beauty around him.

Days turned into weeks. Max explored the island, learning its secrets. He found a cliff that offered a panoramic view and carved a big 'HELP' in the sand on the beach, hoping for rescue.

But Max wasn't just surviving; he was growing. He learned to fish using sharpened sticks and made a small raft for short trips along the coast. He became friends with a curious parrot named Captain, a companion in his solitude.

One day, while exploring the island's far side, Max stumbled upon old ruins, overgrown and forgotten. His heart raced with excitement. The ruins were a puzzle, with carvings that seemed to tell a story. Max spent days deciphering the story, which spoke of ancient travelers and hidden treasures.

As months passed, Max became a true castaway, his skin tanned by the sun, his body strong and agile. He learned to respect the island, understanding that nature was a friend and a formidable force.

Then, Max saw a ship on the horizon on a day that seemed no different from the rest. He ran to his 'HELP' sign, waving frantically. The ship changed course, heading towards the island. Max's heart pounded with a mix of joy and sadness. The island had become a part of him.

The rescue team was amazed by Max's resilience and ingenuity. As Max sailed back to civilization, he realized he was not the same boy who had washed ashore. The island had taught him about survival and, more importantly, the strength within himself.

Back home, reunited with his overjoyed parents, Max often gazed at the sea, remembering his island adventure. He shared his story with others, teaching them the skills he had learned:

1. The importance of finding fresh water and safe food.

2. Building a shelter and learning from nature.

3. The power of hope and the strength of the human spirit.

Max's adventure became a legend in his town, inspiring others with the tale of the boy who became a castaway and found his inner strength on a secret island.

# CHAPTER 3

# The Great Desert Mirage Mystery: Sands, Sun, and Survival Skills - Unraveling desert puzzles under the blazing sun.

A GIRL NAMED AMARA lived in the heart of the vast, sun-kissed desert, where the dunes rose and fell like the waves of a golden sea. Amara's eyes were like the desert sky at dusk, and her spirit was as indomitable as the wind that sculpted the sands. Her home was a small, bustling town on the edge of the desert, where the modern world met ancient traditions.

Amara loved the desert, its mysteries, legends, shifting sands, and hidden treasures. One day, driven by her adventurous heart, she explored the desert to uncover its secrets. She set off into the vast, shimmering wilderness with a backpack filled with essentials – water, a hat, sunglasses, and a compass.

As she ventured more deeply, the desert revealed its harsh beauty. The sun was a fiery chariot racing across the sky and the sands, a scorching blanket beneath her feet. Amara knew the dangers of the desert – the relentless sun, the treacherous mirages, and the water scarcity. But she was prepared, or so she thought.

Hours into her journey, Amara encountered her first challenge – a mirage. What looked like a tranquil lake was just hot air playing tricks on her eyes. She remembered her grandfather's words, "In the desert, your eyes can be your foes; trust your knowledge, not what shows."

Using her compass, Amara navigated, keeping her direction steady. She walked during the more excellent hours and rested in the shade of a dune during the scorching midday sun. As she slept, she often found little desert creatures – a resilient lizard or a swift sand fox – each a marvel of adaptation.

But as the day waned, Amara realized she was lost. The endless dunes looked the same, and her water supply was dwindling. Fear crept into her heart, but she fought it with reason. "To survive is to think," her grandfather used to say.

Remembering his lessons, Amara decided to build a shelter for the night. She found a dune that offered protection from the wind and used her backpack and clothes to create a makeshift shade. As night fell, the desert transformed. The heat gave way to a chilling cold, and the sky lit up with a million stars, each telling its ancient story.

That night, Amara learned the desert's harshest lesson – its unpredictability. She huddled in her shelter, conserving her body heat, and waited for dawn.

With the first light, Amara set out again. She conserved her energy by strolling and taking sips of water regularly. Her goal was to find a high dune to view her surroundings better.

Finally, after hours of struggle, she reached the peak of a tall dune. From there, she saw something glinting in the distance. Using her knowledge of the area and her instinct, she headed towards the glint.

It turned out to be a small, abandoned research station. Inside, she found water and a radio. Amara called for help, giving her coordinates. Rescue came swiftly.

Back in her town, Amara's adventure became a lesson for all. She shared her story, teaching others about the dangers of the desert and how to respect its power:

1. Never underestimate the desert –
   its beauty hides its challenges.

2. Use knowledge and preparation to
   navigate – a compass, understanding of weather patterns, and survival skills.

3. Stay calm and think logically in the
   face of adversity.

While challenging, Amara's journey in the desert had unraveled the mystery of survival in the vast sea of sands. It was a testament to human resilience and the power of knowledge against the might of nature.

CHAPTER 4

# The Blizzard at Broken Ridge: Snow, Stars, and Survival Signals - Braving the frosty fury and the starlit skies.

A BOY NAMED LEO lived in the heart of the icy mountains, where the snow whispers secrets, and the stars dance in the clear night sky. Leo had a heart as warm as a summer day and courage as solid as the mountains he loved. Living in a small, cozy village at the foot of the hills, Leo had always been fascinated by the tales of the high peaks and their mysteries.

One crisp winter morning, fueled by curiosity and bravery, Leo decided to explore Broken Ridge, where, according to village lore, the stars touched the earth. Dressed in his warmest clothes and with a backpack filled with essentials – a flashlight, extra batteries, a map, food, and water – he set off on his adventure.

Leo's journey began under a clear blue sky, but the weather started to change as he ascended. Brooding and ominous clouds gathered, and a chill wind began to howl as if warning Leo of the impending danger. He remembered his father's advice: "In the mountains, respect the weather, for it changes as quickly as a bird takes flight."

As Leo reached the higher slopes of Broken Ridge, a fierce blizzard struck as suddenly as a dragon's roar. The world turned white, and visibility was reduced to mere feet. Leo knew he was in trouble. He needed to find shelter quickly.

Remembering his survival training, Leo used his knowledge of the terrain. He found a rocky outcrop that offered some protection from the howling wind. He created a temporary shelter using his backpack and a large piece of tarp he had brought.

The blizzard raged on, a symphony of wind and snow. Leo realized the importance of staying calm and thinking clearly inside his makeshift shelter. He conserved his energy, eating some of the food he had brought and sipping water slowly.

As night fell, the blizzard showed no signs of stopping. Leo knew he needed to signal for help. He remembered a trick his grandmother had taught him – using a flashlight and a mirror to create a signal visible for miles. He would flash the signal every hour, a beacon of hope amidst the storm.

The night was long and filled with the sounds of the blizzard's fury. But above, the stars watched over Leo, glittering in the gaps of the storm. Leo felt a connection with the vast universe, a sense of being a part of something much larger than himself.

Finally, as the first light of dawn broke, the blizzard started to weaken. A rescue team had seen Leo's signal in the village. As the rescuers approached, Leo felt a wave of relief and pride. He had survived the night, braved the blizzard, and kept his wits about him.

Leo shared his story in the village, warmed by the fire and surrounded by his relieved family. His tale became a lesson for all, teaching them the importance of respecting nature and being prepared:

1. Always appreciate the weather in the mountains and be qualified for sudden changes.

2. Stay calm, use your resources wisely, and think creatively in emergencies.

3. Always remember the value of traditional knowledge and survival skills.

Leo's adventure at Broken Ridge was a tale of survival against the elements and a story of a young boy's resilience, wisdom, and indomitable human spirit under the starlit skies.

# CHAPTER 5

# The Jungle Jamboree Gone Awry: Vines, Venom, and Valiant Ventures - Jungle thrills and the art of avoiding danger.

THERE WAS A BRAVE girl named Maya in a world where the trees danced to the tune of the wind and the rivers sang songs of ancient times. Maya's hair was as wild as the jungle she loved, and her spirit was as free as the birds that soared above it. Her village, a tapestry of huts and laughter, lay on the edge of a vast, mysterious jungle.

Maya heard tales of the jungle, its hidden wonders, and secret paths. She dreamed of exploring it and experiencing its untamed beauty. One day, driven by her adventurous heart and insatiable curiosity, Maya decided to delve into the jungle's depths and become part of its untold stories.

Armed with a backpack filled with essentials – a first-aid kit, water, a whistle, and a sturdy rope – Maya stepped into the green embrace of the jungle. The canopy above was a kaleidoscope of greens, and the air was alive with the calls of exotic birds and unseen creatures.

As Maya ventured more profoundly, the jungle revealed its mesmerizing beauty and lurking dangers. She navigated through thick underbrush and over tangled roots, her eyes wide with wonder and caution. She knew the jungle was a land of marvels and perils – from venomous snakes to hidden pitfalls.

Her first test came when she encountered a river, its waters swift and murky. Remembering her father's teachings, Maya used her rope to create a makeshift bridge, testing each step before moving forward. Her heart raced with excitement as she crossed the river, a triumphant smile on her lips.

But as the day wore on, Maya realized she had wandered too far. The familiar landmarks of her village were nowhere in sight. Fear gripped her heart, but she remembered her mother's words, "In the heart of the jungle, your wits are your best companion."

Maya decided to climb a tall tree to get a better view. From the top, she saw the vastness of the jungle, a never-ending sea of green. But she also spotted smoke rising in the distance – a sign of her village.

Descending the tree, Maya started toward the smoke. She marked her path by tying pieces of brightly colored cloth to branches. The jungle was a maze, but she was determined to maintain her way.

As night approached, the jungle transformed. The air filled with the symphony of nocturnal creatures, and the darkness seemed to have a life of its own. Maya found a safe spot to rest, high in a tree, away from the reach of prowling animals.

That night, under a tapestry of stars, Maya learned the most crucial lesson – respect for the jungle and its inhabitants. She understood she was a small part of this vast, wild world.

With the first light of dawn, guided by the smoke and her markers, Maya finally emerged from the jungle. Her village greeted her with cheers and relief. Maya shared her adventure, her eyes sparkling with the thrill of it all.

Her story became a lesson for the village, especially for the young ones, teaching them about the wonders and dangers of the jungle:

1. Always be prepared and respect the untamed nature of the jungle.

2. Use your knowledge and instincts to navigate and make intelligent decisions.

3. Understand the importance of leaving markers and having a plan.

Maya's adventure in the jungle was more than just a journey; it was a rite of passage, a testament to her courage, wisdom, and the eternal dance between humans and nature.

# CHAPTER 6

# A drift in the Open Sea: Waves, Whales, and Water Wisdom - Ocean odyssey and the secrets of the deep blue.

A BOY NAMED FINN lived in a quaint coastal town where the sea sang lullabies at night, and the air tasted of salt and freedom. Finn had dreams as vast as the ocean and a yearning for adventure as deep as the sea. His father was a fisherman, and Finn had learned to love and respect the mighty ocean from him.

One sunny day, driven by a spirit of adventure and the tales of mariners, Finn decided to venture into the open sea. He prepared his small boat, including essentials like a life jacket, flares, a compass, and plenty of water and food.

As Finn sailed from the shore, the land became a distant memory, and the sea stretched around him like a giant, blue canvas. The ocean was a world of its own, with rolling waves and breezes that spoke of faraway places.

But the sea, as Finn knew, was unpredictable. Without warning, a storm gathered. The sky darkened, and the waves rose like angry giants. Finn's boat was tossed around, and he lost his oars and direction in the chaos. When the storm finally passed, Finn found himself adrift in the vastness of the open sea, alone and with no land in sight.

Fear gripped Finn's heart, but he remembered his father's words, "In the heart of the sea, your wits are your sail, your courage, your anchor." Taking a deep breath, Finn assessed his situation. He had limited supplies, but if rationed carefully, they could last.

Finn scanned the horizon daily for signs of land or ships. He used his knowledge of the stars to try to navigate, keeping his spirits up by talking to the seagulls and dolphins that occasionally accompanied him.

Finn also utilized his resources creatively. He fashioned a fishing line out of some spare rope and a hook he found in his boat, catching fish for food. He collected rainwater to supplement his water supply.

One day, while adrift, Finn witnessed a magnificent sight – a pod of whales, majestic and awe-inspiring. They swam close to his boat, and for a moment, Finn felt a connection with these giants of the deep, a feeling of being part of something larger than himself.

As days turned into weeks, Finn's hope started to wane. But he kept his routine, his rationing, and his vigilance. His survival depended not just on his physical resources but also on his mental strength.

Finally, one fateful morning, Finn's persistence paid off. A ship appeared on the horizon. He used his flares to signal, and the ship altered its course towards him. Finn was rescued.

Finn's story of survival on the open sea became a legend in his town. He shared his tale and the lessons he learned:

1. The importance of being prepared for the unpredictability of the sea.

2. The value of resourcefulness and rationing in survival situations.

3. The power of hope and mental strength in the face of adversity.

Finn's journey was more than a test of survival; it was a voyage of self-discovery and a testament to the resilience of the human spirit amidst the waves and the vast, mysterious blue.

# CHAPTER 7

# The Cave of Echoes: Stalactites, Shadows, and Subterranean Secrets - Underground marvels and echoes of mystery.

IN A TOWN WHERE the hills hugged the sky and the streams whispered old tales, a girl named Lily was as curious as a cat and brave as a lion. Lily's backyard was a playground of hills and caves, each one whispering secrets of a hidden world beneath.

One day, armed with a spirit of adventure (and a flashlight), Lily explored the most mysterious Cave of Echoes. The cave said to be a labyrinth of wonders, had fascinated Lily since she was as small as a hobbit.

Before venturing into the cave, Lily prepared like a true explorer. She packed her backpack with essentials – a flashlight, extra batteries, a map of the cave (drawn by a local explorer who loved riddles), snacks, and a sturdy rope. She even wore her lucky hat, which was as colorful as a parrot's wings.

As Lily stepped into the cave, the world transformed. Stalactites hung from the ceiling like nature's chandeliers, and the air was as cool as a cucumber in a fridge. The cave's walls echoed Lily's every step as if they were chatting with her.

Lily used her map, which was as puzzling as a crossword puzzle, to navigate the maze of tunnels. The deeper she went, the more the cave revealed its secrets. There were crystal-clear pools mirrored the ceiling like gateways to another world and rocks that sparkled like diamonds at a ball.

But as Lily explored, she realized she had wandered off the map's path. The cave, like a giant maze, had tricked her. She found herself in a large, echoing chamber with no apparent way out. Like an uninvited guest at a party, a tinge of fear crept into her heart.

However, Lily remembered her grandfather's words, "When you're in a pickle, use your noodle." She took a deep breath and observed her surroundings. The cave, she realized, was like a giant puzzle, and she loved puzzles.

Lily noticed that the echoes in the cave changed depending on the direction she faced. Using her sharp ears and the echoes as her guide, she started to find her way back. She marked her path by drawing arrows with a piece of chalk she had brought, creating a breadcrumb trail as Hansel and Gretel did, but without the fear of a witch.

The journey back was like a game of hot and cold. Each echo guided her, telling her if she was getting "warmer" or "colder." Finally, after what felt like a chess game with the cave, Lily returned to the entrance.

Stepping out of the cave, Lily was greeted by the warm embrace of the sun, like a mother hugging her child after a long day. She had explored the Cave of Echoes and outsmarted its labyrinth.

Back home, Lily shared her adventure, her eyes twinkling with the thrill of it. She taught the town's children about the wonders beneath their feet and the importance of using their senses and wit:

1. Be prepared and respect the mystery of nature's creations.

2. Use your observation skills and logic to navigate complex situations.

3. Learn to rely on different senses – in this case, listening to the echoes.

Lily's adventure in the Cave of Echoes be-
came a celebrated tale in her town, a story of curiosity, courage, and the joy of
solving nature's riddles.

# CHAPTER 8

# The Mountain that Whispered: Peaks, Paths, and Puzzling Trails - Scaling heights and decoding nature's whispers.

THERE LIVED A BOY named Ethan in a quaint village nestled in the embrace of towering mountains, where eagles soared high, and secrets lay hidden in misty veils. Ethan's hair was as wild as the mountain winds, and his dreams were as tall as the peaks that kissed the sky. He often gazed at the mountains, imagining them as ancient guardians whispering age-old secrets.

One clear morning, with a backpack slung over his shoulders and a heart full of determination, Ethan set out to unravel the mystery of the Whispering Mountain – a peak said to hold the wisdom of the ages. He packed his bag like a treasure chest, with a map, compass, water, snacks, and a warm jacket – just in case the mountain decided to play a game of freeze-tag.

As Ethan began his ascent, the mountain seemed to greet him with open arms. Birds chirped as if cheering him on, and the trees rustled in a chorus of whispers. The path wound upwards like a serpent playing hide and seek with the sun.

The higher Ethan climbed, the more he felt the mountain's mystical aura. It was as if each rock and tree had a story to tell, and Ethan was there to listen. But as the path grew steeper, the skies decided to play a little prank. Clouds gathered, gray and grumbling, and soon, a fog as thick as Grandma's pea soup enveloped Ethan.

Standing amidst the swirling mists, Ethan felt like he had entered a cloud kingdom. But the path became a puzzle, with the fog playing the role of a mischievous jester. Ethan's map was as helpful as a chocolate teapot in this soup of fog.

Remembering his grandfather's old mountain tales, Ethan decided to use his other senses. He listened for the sound of a stream marked on his map – streams, after all, don't play hide and seek with the fog. Following the gurgling sound of a detective following clues, Ethan managed to stay on the right path.

As hours passed, Ethan's journey became a dance with the mountain. The fog lifted occasionally, giving him glimpses of the path, only to swoop down again, giggling like a naughty child. But Ethan persisted, his determination as unyielding as the mountain itself.

Finally, as the sun started to dip, painting the sky with strokes of oranges and pinks, Ethan reached the summit. The view was like a giant painting, with the world stretched below. The mountain whispered its secrets to him – secrets of resilience, beauty, and the harmony of nature.

Ethan spent some time at the summit, talking to the mountain like an old friend. He realized the journey was more than just reaching the top and understanding the mountain's silent language.

As night approached, Ethan descended, the mountain's whispers echoing in his heart. He reached the village under a blanket of stars, his eyes shining with the wisdom of his adventure.

Ethan shared his tale with the villagers, his story becoming a tapestry of humor, courage, and the voice of nature:

1. In the face of challenges, use all your senses and intuition.

2. The journey is as important as the destination, filled with lessons and wonders.

3. Nature speaks silently; learning to listen can reveal its deepest secrets.

Ethan's adventure on the Whispering Mountain became a legend in his village. It is the story of a boy who conversed with the mountain and learned its ancient whispers.

# CHAPTER 9

# The Labyrinth of the Lost City: Ruins, Riddles, and Urban Resilience - A concrete jungle adventure wrapped in history.

IN A WORLD WHERE skyscrapers brushed the clouds and streets buzzed with the symphony of city life, there lived a girl named Ava. Ava's mind was as sharp as a Sherlock Holmes novel, and her curiosity was as boundless as the universe. She lived in a bustling city, but her heart yearned for mysteries and secrets in forgotten corners.

One day, inspired by tales of ancient cities and lost civilizations, Ava set out on an urban adventure. She aimed to unravel the mystery of the Lost City, an old part of town, now a labyrinth of abandoned buildings and overgrown alleys said to hold past secrets.

Ava prepared for her expedition like Indiana Jones on a quest. She packed a backpack with essentials – a flashlight, a notebook, a camera, and a map of the city. She even wore a hat that made her feel like a true explorer.

As she delved into the heart of the Lost City, the modern world seemed to fade away. Once, tall and proud buildings stood like ancient ruins, their walls telling stories of days gone by. The streets were a maze, each turn leading to another mystery.

Ava felt like she was walking through the pages of a history book. She explored old buildings, each room whispering tales of the past. She found old newspapers, photographs, and artifacts, each a piece of a puzzle she was eager to solve.

Ava ventured deeper and realized the Lost City's labyrinth was more complex than she had anticipated. The map was helpful, but the city had changed. Streets that once existed were gone, replaced by dead ends and new paths.

It was like playing chess with history. Ava had to think two steps ahead, anticipate changes, and adapt her route. She used her knowledge of the city's history to navigate and understand how the past shaped the present.

The Lost City, however, had challenges. The floors were treacherous, and the scurry of unseen creatures occasionally broke the silence. But Ava's spirit was undaunted. Her adventure was not just a physical journey but a journey through time.

As the day turned to dusk, Ava found herself in the heart of the Lost City – a grand old plaza now reclaimed by nature. It was as if time had stopped, waiting for someone to hear its story.

Ava discovered what she had been searching for in the plaza – a mural, hidden away from the world, telling the story of the city's glorious past. It was like finding a treasure chest in an attic. Ava documented her findings, her heart racing with the thrill of discovery.

With night approaching, Ava made her way back to the modern world. The city lights welcomed her like twinkling stars on Earth. She returned home, her mind buzzing with ideas and her camera full of memories.

Ava shared her adventure and discoveries, her story captivating everyone:

1. The importance of understanding and respecting our history and heritage.

2. The skills of navigation, problem-solving, and adaptation in unfamiliar environments.

3. The thrill of exploration and the joy of uncovering hidden stories.

Ava's journey through the Labyrinth of the Lost City became an inspiring tale in her city, a reminder of the hidden mysteries waiting to be discovered just around the corner.

# CHAPTER 10

# The Unexpected Flash Flood: Rivers, Rains, and Rapid Responses - A deluge of danger and the race against time.

IN A SMALL, PEACEFUL town where the river wound through like a silver ribbon and the hills watched over like gentle giants, there lived a boy named Noah. Noah smiled like a burst of sunshine and a knack for making the best out of any situation, much like a magician turning a scarf into a dove.

One warm, seemingly ordinary day, Noah decided to hike along the river trail, a path he knew as well as the back of his hand. He set off with a backpack containing a water bottle, snacks, and a trusty first-aid kit, whistling a tune that danced with the birds' songs.

As Noah walked, admiring the river's peaceful flow and the way the trees swayed in a lazy dance with the breeze, dark clouds began to gather overhead, like uninvited guests at a picnic. Within moments, the sky turned into a canvas of gray, and rain poured down as if someone had overturned a giant bucket in the heavens.

Though surprised by the sudden change, Noah found shelter under a large tree. He expected the rain to be a brief visitor, but the downpour grew stronger. The river, usually as calm as a sleeping cat, began to swell and roar like a lion awakened.

Realizing the situation was turning serious, Noah remembered the flash flood warnings he had learned in school. He knew he had to move to higher ground immediately. This was no longer a gentle hike but a race against the rising waters.

Noah began his trek towards the hills, with the rain blurring his vision like a foggy window. The path, once clear, was now a muddy obstacle course. He moved cautiously but with the urgency of a squirrel saving nuts for the winter.

As he climbed, the sounds of the river turned ominous. It was as if the water was chasing him, eager to engulf everything in its path. The ground beneath his feet became increasingly treacherous, each step a battle against the slippery mud.

But Noah was not one to be easily defeated. He used branches for support, like a mountaineer using his pick, and navigated through the increasingly dense underbrush. His heart pounded in his chest, a drumbeat that echoed the river's rush.

Finally, after what seemed like an eternity, Noah reached the safety of higher ground. He turned to look back at the river, now a raging beast where a serene stream once flowed. He had escaped the flood, but seeing the transformed landscape was a stark reminder of nature's unpredictable power.

Exhausted but safe, Noah awaited the rescue teams, which arrived as the rain surrendered to the returning sun. He was hailed as a hero, a young boy who had shown courage and quick thinking in the face of danger.

Back in town, Noah shared his story, emphasizing the lessons he learned:

1. Awareness of weather changes and natural disaster warnings is important.

2. The need for quick thinking and immediate action in emergencies.

3. The value of knowledge and pre-paredness in ensuring personal safety.

Noah's experience with the unexpected flash flood became a lesson for the town, a story of resilience, respect for nature, and the power of the presence of mind.

# Chapter 11

# The Fire in the Foothills: Flames, Forethought, and Fiery Escapes - Wildfire woes and lessons in prevention.

IN A TOWN CRADLED by foothills and forests, where the air smelled of pine and adventure, there lived a girl named Emma. Emma had a spirit as vibrant as a wildfire and a heart brave enough to match. She was as curious about the forests surrounding her town as a cat is about a new box.

One dry, windy afternoon, Emma decided to explore the foothills, where trees stood tall like guardians of ancient secrets. With a backpack equipped with water, a sandwich, a whistle, and her trusty binoculars, she set off, her steps as light as a deer's.

As she trekked, Emma reveled in the beauty of the woods. The birds sang their afternoon songs, and the leaves rustled in a symphony of whispers. But amidst this harmony, Emma noticed something unusual – a wisp of smoke rising in the distance, as out of place as a snowman in the desert.

Remembering the fire safety drills from school, Emma's heart raced with fear and adrenaline. She knew even a tiny spark could dance into a raging wildfire in the dry season. She grabbed her binoculars, and through them, she saw the early signs of a small but hungry fire creeping through the underbrush.

Emma knew she had to act fast. The fire was small enough to be missed by the distant watch towers but big enough to become a menace. She took out her whistle and blew it three times – the signal for danger.

Then, with the wisdom of a seasoned ranger, Emma began making her way back to town, choosing a path that kept the wind and the fire's potential path at her back. Her journey back was no stroll in the woods; it was a strategic retreat, a race against an invisible enemy.

As she moved, Emma kept an eye on the smoke. The wind was picking up as if it wanted to join forces with the fire. Emma's knowledge of the area was her compass – she avoided areas with dense underbrush and took routes that were less likely to be in the fire's path.

Finally, after what felt like a marathon trek, Emma emerged from the woods into the safety of her town. She immediately alerted the fire department. Thanks to her timely warning, the firefighters could contain the fire before it could threaten the city.

Emma's quick thinking and bravery became the talk of the town. She shared her story, emphasizing the lessons she had learned:

1. The importance of being alert and recognizing the early signs of wild-fires.

2. The need for quick, calm deci-sion-making in emergencies.

3. The value of knowing your envi-ronment and the basics of fire safe-ty.

Emma's encounter with the fire in the foothills became a testament to her courage and a lesson on the importance of fire awareness and safety in nature.

# CHAPTER 12

# The Tornado's Twist: Winds, Whirls, and Weathering the Storm - Spiraling into the eye of the storm and outsmarting it.

A BOY NAMED JACK lived in a small town where the fields stretched like green oceans and the sky often told stories with its clouds. Jack had hair as unruly as a summer storm and a curiosity that could outmatch a cat's. Like a sky with many faces, he had always been fascinated by the weather, its moods, and tantrums.

One sultry afternoon, the air changed as Jack played in his backyard. It became heavy, like a blanket too thick for comfort. The sky turned a menacing shade of green, and the clouds raced as if late for a meeting. Jack's heart leaped – he recognized these signs. A tornado was brewing, a giant of wind and might, ready to dance its destructive dance.

With no time to waste, Jack sprinted into his house. He remembered the drills and the advice from weather safety classes – in a tornado; the basement was the safest place. He gathered his family, including his little sister, Lily, who clung to her teddy bear like a life raft.

As they hurried to the basement, Jack grabbed the emergency kit they had prepared – a flashlight, batteries, water, food, and a first-aid kit. They huddled together, listening to the roar of the wind like a freight train charging through their world.

Jack tried to calm Lily by telling her stories. He spun tales of brave knights and clever wizards, his voice a steady rhythm against the drumming of the storm. He knew that staying calm was as important as any physical shelter.

The tornado raged outside, a beast throwing its weight around. It uprooted trees and tossed objects as if they were mere toys. But in the basement, Jack and his family were safe, a little island amid chaos.

After what seemed like hours, the storm passed. They emerged from their shelter like survivors of a great battle. The sight that greeted them was one of devastation. The tornado had left its mark, a signature of destruction. But amidst the chaos, there was a sense of relief and gratitude. They were safe, and that was what mattered.

Jack became a little hero in his town in the days that followed. His foresight to take shelter and calm during the storm kept his family safe. He shared his experience and the lessons he had learned:

1. Recognizing the signs of severe weather and acting quickly is important.

2. There needs to be a plan and an emergency kit ready for such situations.

3. The power of staying calm and providing emotional support during crises.

Jack's encounter with the tornado's twist became a story of courage, resilience, and the importance of being prepared for nature's unpredictable moods.

CHAPTER 13

# The Quake that Shook the Town: Tremors, Traps, and Tenacious Tactics - Shaking up survival skills when the earthquakes.

I N A COZY TOWN nestled between rolling hills and whispering woods, where every street held memories, and every corner told a story, a girl named Sophie lived. Sophie had eyes as bright as a new day and a courage that never seemed to wane, even in the face of the unknown.

One quiet evening, the unimaginable happened as Sophie was working on her school project. Without warning, the ground beneath her feet began to dance a terrifying tango. Like a distant thunderstorm, it started as a low rumble but quickly grew into a monstrous roar. Like an uninvited monster from deep within the earth, the earthquake had arrived.

Sophie remembered her earthquake drills. She ducked under her sturdy desk, her little fortress amidst the chaos. Around her, the world shook as if in the grip of an angry giant. Books tumbled from shelves, pictures leaped off the walls, and the lights flickered like a candle in the wind.

As the tremors continued, Sophie's heart raced. But amidst the fear, she found a sliver of calm. She knew that staying put and protecting her head was crucial.

The desk was her island in a stormy sea, and she clung to it like a shipwrecked sailor to a lifeboat.

Finally, after what seemed like an eternity, the shaking stopped. Sophie emerged from her makeshift shelter, a little shaken but unharmed. She quickly checked herself for injuries, a self-assessment like a detective looking for clues.

The house was a mess, a jigsaw puzzle thrown into disarray. Sophie knew she had to be careful – aftershocks were like the earthquake's mischievous siblings, ready to strike without notice. She put on her sturdy shoes to protect her feet from broken glass, a lesson she remembered from her emergency preparedness classes.

Her next step was to check on her family and neighbors. The town, usually a picture of tranquility, was now a scene of confusion and alarm. Sophie moved with purpose, her steps careful but confident.

As she navigated the town, helping where she could, Sophie became a beacon of hope and resilience. She supported an elderly neighbor turn off the gas to prevent a potential fire, a danger as sneaky as a thief in the night. She provided first aid to a young boy with a minor cut, her hands as steady as a surgeon's.

The earthquake had indeed shaken the town, but it also brought the community together. People helped each other, sharing resources and supporting, a tapestry of unity and strength.

In the aftermath, Sophie shared her story and the lessons she learned:

1. The importance of staying calm and taking cover during an earthquake.

2. There is a need for self-assessment and being aware of potential aftershocks.

3. The value of community support and helping each other in times of crisis.

Sophie's experience during the quake that shook the town became a testament to her bravery and a reminder of the importance of being prepared and coming together in the face of adversity.

49

# CHAPTER 14

# The Avalanche Adventure: Snow, Secrets, and Survival Signals - The snowy slide and the quest for safe passage.

A BOY NAMED LUCAS lived in a small village, cradled by snow-capped mountains and blanketed under a sky as blue as a robin's egg. Lucas had an adventurous spirit that matched the vastness of the mountains and a curiosity as endless as the winding trails.

One crisp winter morning, Lucas, equipped with his love for the mountains and a backpack filled with essentials – a thermal flask, extra gloves, a first-aid kit, and an avalanche transceiver – set out to conquer the snowy trails. His heart was light, and his steps were as excited as a puppy's.

As Lucas ascended, the world transformed into a winter wonderland. The snow-covered trees stood like silent sentinels, and the air was crisp and clear as if freshly washed. But as he ventured more profoundly, the weather suddenly turned like a plot twist in a mystery novel. The sky darkened, and the wind howled as if singing an ominous lullaby.

Aware of the mountain's fickle nature, Lucas decided to head back. But as he turned, he heard a sound – a low rumble, like distant thunder. His heart skipped a beat. It was an avalanche cascading down the mountain with the fury of a thousand horses.

In seconds, Lucas's adventure turned into a survival mission. He knew the drill – he had to move sideways to the avalanche path as swiftly as a fox dodging a hunter. The avalanche, like a white dragon, was fast and unforgiving.

Lucas made a dash to the side with his avalanche transceiver in hand. The snow surged around him, a cold, relentless wave. He used his ski poles to propel himself, each push a battle against the snow's grip.

When he thought he was out of danger, the snow enveloped him, pulling him into its cold embrace. Buried under the snow, Lucas fought to stay calm. He created an air pocket and used his whistle, blowing it in bursts of three – the universal signal for help.

Meanwhile, his transceiver sent out signals, a technological cry for help. Time was a luxury he didn't have. Under the snow, minutes he stretched like hours. Lucas's thoughts went to his family, a flicker of warmth in the cold darkness.

Above the snow, the rescue team, alerted by his transceiver signal, worked tirelessly. With shovels and probes, they were like detectives searching for a clue. Finally, they located Lucas. The rescue was swift, and as they pulled him out, the air never tasted sweeter.

Lucas's brush with the avalanche became a story of resilience and survival. In the warmth of his home, surrounded by his relieved family, he shared his harrowing experience and the lessons he learned:

1. The importance of respecting nature and being aware of the risks, especially in avalanche-prone areas.

2. The necessity of carrying the right equipment and knowing survival techniques.

3. The power of hope and the critical role of rescue teams in emergencies.

Though difficult, Lucas's avalanche adventure became a testament to his courage and a reminder of the awe-inspiring yet dangerous beauty of the mountains.

# CHAPTER 15

# The Great Coral Reef Challenge: Safe Snorkeling and Respecting Marine Life - Underwater wonders and respecting the reef.

THERE LIVED A GIRL named Mia in a coastal town kissed by the sun and serenaded by the waves. Mia loved the ocean as deep as the sea and a curiosity as vibrant as the colorful corals that adorned the ocean bed. Her dream was to explore the underwater kingdom, swim with the fish, and speak the language of the waves.

One sunny morning, Mia decided to take on the Great Coral Reef Challenge – a snorkeling adventure to explore the magnificent coral reefs just off the coast. Equipped with her snorkeling gear, an underwater camera, and a heart full of excitement, she set out on her aquatic adventure.

Mia entered a world unlike any other as she plunged into the clear blue waters. The coral reef was a kaleidoscope of colors, a living, breathing masterpiece. Fish of all shapes and sizes darted around her as if she were a guest in their underwater castle.

Mia was in awe. The corals were like underwater gardens, with anemones waving their tentacles like tiny dancers and clownfish playing hide and seek among them. She remembered her promise to respect the marine life and not touch the corals, aware that her fingers could be knights causing unintended havoc in this fragile kingdom.

But as Mia ventured further, she noticed something troubling. Parts of the reef were damaged, bleached white like bones in the sun. It was a stark reminder that this underwater paradise was vulnerable, a treasure chest that needed guarding.

Mia decided to document her findings. She took photos and made mental notes, her camera a tool for storytelling, her mind an archive of this underwater saga. She knew sharing these images could help raise awareness about the reef's fragility.

As she swam back to the shore, Mia felt mixed emotions. The reef's beauty had filled her with joy, but its vulnerability had left a mark on her heart. She was determined to be a voice for the ocean, a storyteller for the silent creatures below the waves.

Back on land, Mia shared her experience and her photos. She talked about the vibrant life on the reef and the importance of protecting it. She became an advocate for the ocean, urging others to respect and preserve its wonders:

1. The importance of responsible snorkeling – admiring marine life without disturbing it.

2. There is a need to raise awareness about the health of coral reefs and the ocean.

3. The power of individual action in contributing to the conservation of marine ecosystems.

Mia's adventure in the Great Coral Reef became more than just a snorkeling journey; it was a mission to protect and cherish the underwater world, a testament to the beauty of the ocean and the responsibility we all share in preserving it.

# CHAPTER 16

# The Hike through Haunted Hills: Fog, Folklore, and Fearless Footsteps - A trek through tales and twilight mysteries.

A BOY NAMED ETHAN lived in a quaint village, nestled in the embrace of rolling hills shrouded in myths and mist. Ethan had a curiosity as boundless as the starry sky and a love for adventures that rivaled the greatest explorers. The Haunted Hills had always captured his imagination with their veils of fog and whispering winds.

One chilly autumn morning, Ethan, armed with a backpack filled with essentials – a flashlight, a map, a compass, snacks, and a warm jacket – set out to explore the Haunted Hills. With their gnarled trees and ancient stones, the hills were said to be home to spirits and secrets from the long past.

As Ethan began his hike, the hills welcomed him with a carpet of fallen leaves and a symphony of rustling branches. The fog hung low, like a ghostly curtain waiting to be unveiled. Ethan's heart thumped with excitement and a hint of fear – after all, he was stepping into the pages of the village's bedtime stories. The more bottomless Ethan ventured, the thicker the fog became. It swirled around him like a mystical dance, obscuring the path and playing tricks on his eyes. Shadows seemed to move, and the wind appeared to carry voices from another time.

But Ethan was not easily frightened. He remembered his grandfather's words, "In the land of folklore, fear is the traveler's greatest enemy." Holding onto his sense of adventure, Ethan used his compass and map to navigate, his every step a note in this eerie melody.

As he trekked through the hills, Ethan encountered remnants of the past – an old, abandoned cabin with stories etched into its walls and a forgotten well, its waters as still as the air. He felt like a detective uncovering clues from a forgotten world.

But as the day wore on, the fog grew so dense that it was like walking through a cloud. Ethan realized he needed to head back before darkness fell and turned the hills into a maze of shadows.  Using his compass and the map, he retraced his steps. The journey back was a test of his memory and instincts. Every rock and tree seemed like a landmark, yet nothing was inevitable in the fog. It was like playing a game of memory, where the stakes were as high as the thrill.

Finally, after what seemed like an eternity, the fog began to lift, revealing the familiar path leading back to the village. Ethan emerged from the Haunted Hills with a sense of accomplishment. He had walked the land of legends and returned, his heart brimming with stories and his mind with memories.

Back in the village, Ethan became a little hero. He shared his adventure, telling tales of the eerie beauty and the whispers in the fog. He spoke of courage and the importance of trusting one's instincts:

1. The significance of preparation and using tools like maps and compasses.

2. The value of facing fears and the thrill of exploring the unknown.

3. The importance of respecting local legends while seeking one's truth.

Ethan's hike through the Haunted Hills became a story passed down in the village, a tale of bravery, mystery, and the eternal dance between legend and adventure.

# CHAPTER 17

# The Cyclone at Sea: Gales, Gusts, and Navigating the Tempest - Riding the waves of wrath and wisdom.

IN A COASTAL TOWN where the sea whispered tales of yore and the horizon kissed the sky, there lived a young sailor named Alex. Alex had a heart that yearned for the sea's vast mysteries and a soul as brave as old mariners. The sea was his playground, his teacher, and his greatest challenge.

One fateful day, with the sun shining like a gold coin in the sky, Alex set out on a solo sailing adventure. His sturdy vessel, 'The Nomad,' was equipped with essentials – a radio, navigation tools, food, water, and an emergency kit. Alex, with a spirit as buoyant as his boat, was ready to conquer the seas.

The ocean revealed its many faces as Alex sailed further from the shore. The gentle waves were like playful dolphins, and the breeze sang songs of distant lands. But the sea, a master of disguise, soon turned. Dark clouds rolled in like an army of shadows, and the wind howled like a pack of wolves.

An unannounced and furious cyclone was upon Alex. The sea transformed into a tumultuous beast, its waves towering like skyscrapers. Alex's heart pounded against his chest, a drumbeat in the chaos.

But fear, though a natural stowaway, was not the captain of this ship. Alex remembered his father's teachings, "In the heart of the storm, your wits are your compass." He knew he had to stay calm and think clearly.

First, he secured himself with a safety harness, knowing the sea was no place for a careless dance. Then, he reduced the sails, not wanting to challenge the wind to a duel it would surely win. His movements were deliberate, each step a calculated chess move against the storm.

Alex skillfully and determinedly steered "The Nomad' through the cyclone. He kept the bow pointed into the waves, riding them like a bronco rider up and down the watery hills and valleys. The boat creaked and groaned, a symphony of survival against nature's might.

Throughout the night, Alex battled the storm. His body was weary, but his spirit was unyielding. He spoke to the sea, his voice a mix of defiance and respect: "You may challenge me, but you will not defeat me."

When dawn broke, the storm had passed. The sea, like a tired warrior, calmed its fury. The sky cleared, revealing a canvas of soft blues and gentle pinks. Alex, though exhausted, felt a surge of triumph. He had weathered the cyclone, a testament to his courage and skill.

Upon his return, Alex's tale became a legend in the town. He shared his story not as a tale of conquest but as a lesson in respect for nature's power:

1. The importance of preparation and understanding the weather at sea.

2. The necessity of staying calm and using one's knowledge in the face of danger.

3. The power of respect for the sea and its unpredictable nature.

Alex's adventure with the cyclone at sea was more than a story of survival; it was a narrative of a sailor's reverence for the ocean and the wisdom gained in its wildest moments.

# CHAPTER 18

# The Volcano's Secret: Lava, Legends, and Life Lessons - The fiery giant's whispers and survival strategies.

THERE LIVED A GIRL named Isla in a vibrant town nestled in the shadow of a slumbering volcano, where tales of fire and brimstone were as familiar as the flowers that bloomed in its soil. Isla had a mind as bright as the lava that flowed deep beneath the earth and a spirit as fiery as the volcano.

One crisp morning, Isla, armed with her adventurous heart and a backpack filled with essentials – a map, water, a flashlight, and a geology book – set out to explore the volcano, a towering figure of mystery and power. Her goal was to understand the giant, to listen to its silent stories.

As Isla trekked up the volcano's slopes, the earth beneath her feet was like a sleeping dragon, peaceful yet formidable. The volcano, with its lush slopes and whispering vents, was a world of nurturing and destructive contrasts.

But as Isla ventured further, the ground trembled – a low rumble, like the earth's heartbeat. She felt a thrill of fear and excitement. The volcano was speaking, and she was there to listen. She remembered her mother's words, "Nature speaks in many ways, but we must be wise enough to understand."

Isla knew the dangers of being close to an active volcano. She was careful to stay on marked trails and away from steaming vents or fissures.

Her map was a treasure guide, leading her through the safest paths, away from the volcano's hidden traps.

The higher Isla climbed, the more the volcano revealed. She saw vents releasing steam as if the mountain was breathing. She found rocks formed by ancient lava flows, each a story of fiery births. She felt like a detective uncovering the secrets of a giant.

But then, the unexpected happened. The volcano awoke with a start, like a giant disturbed from its sleep. A plume of ash and steam erupted into the sky, painting it gray. Isla'sIsla's heart raced. It was time to put her knowledge to the test.

She quickly donned her protective mask, shielding herself from the ash. Then, she began her descent using her map and understanding of the wind's direction. Her steps were quick but measured, each move a calculated decision.

As she descended, the volcano's rumble was a constant companion. But Isla was not deterred. Her respect for the volcano's power and her understanding of its language guided her down.

Finally, after a descent that tested her resolve and knowledge, Isla reached the town's safety. The volcano continued to rumble in the distance, a reminder of the earth's untamed spirit.

Back in her town, Isla's adventure became a lesson for all. She shared her story, emphasizing the importance of understanding and respecting nature:

1. There is a need to appreciate the power of natural phenomena like volcanoes.

2. The importance of preparation and knowledge of the natural world.

3. The value of listening to nature's signs and acting wisely in the face of danger.

Isla's journey to the heart of the volcano was more than an adventure; it was a dance with one of nature's most potent forces, a testament to her bravery and the awe-inspiring power of the earth.

CHAPTER 19

# The Oasis Mirage: Dunes, Dreams, and Desert Discoveries - A desert quest for truth in a sea of sand.

IN A LAND WHERE the sun ruled the sky with a fiery fist and the dunes rolled like waves in a vast, sandy sea, there lived a boy named Samir. Samir's eyes sparkled like stars in the desert night, and his thirst for adventure was as unquenchable as the desert's thirst for rain.

Driven by tales of lost cities and hidden oases, Samir embarked on a journey across the desert. With a backpack filled with essentials – water, a wide-brimmed hat, a compass, and a map – he set off into the heart of the golden wilderness. His heart beat in rhythm with the shifting sands, each step a note in a song of exploration.

As Samir traversed the desert, the sun was a relentless overseer, its rays a cascade of heat. The dunes were like giant sculptures, changing shapes with the whims of the wind. Samir felt like a sailor navigating an ocean of sand, each dune a wave to conquer.

But the desert, a master of illusions, soon presented its challenge. In the distance, Samir spotted an oasis, a haven of palm trees and water. Excitement surged through him like a river in flood. Could this be the hidden oasis of legend?

Driven by curiosity and hope, Samir followed the mirage. But as he drew closer, the vision of water and trees dissolved into the hot air, a dream melting in the sun. It was a mirage, a trick of the desert, as elusive as a shadow in the night.

Samir felt a momentary pang of disappointment, but his spirit remained undaunted. He realized that the desert's greatest lesson was not about finding an oasis but about understanding the mirage. The desert was teaching him about mirages – not just the ones you see, but also the ones you feel.

Samir set up camp as the day turned to evening, and the sun softened its gaze. The desert night was a kingdom of stars, a tapestry of twinkling lights woven by an unseen hand. Samir lay under the starlit sky, the sand his bed, the stars his companions.

The following day, Samir continued his journey. He had learned to differentiate between the mirages and the natural signs of the desert. He followed the tracks of animals, knowing that they often led to natural water sources. His journey was across the desert and into the depths of understanding and survival.

After days of travel, Samir's perseverance paid off. He found an oasis, but not the one of legend. It was smaller, a hidden gem cradled by the dunes. It was natural, with water that sparkled in the sun and trees that whispered secrets of the desert.

Samir returned to his village, his journey an odyssey of discovery. He shared his story, teaching others about the desert's wonders and deceits:

1. The importance of understanding and respecting the desert environment.

2. The skill of distinguishing between illusion and reality in challenging situations.

3. The value of perseverance and the lessons learned in the pursuit of dreams.

Samir's quest for the Oasis Mirage became a tale of adventure and wisdom, a journey through the desert and the mirages of life.

# CHAPTER 20

# The Riddle of the Rainforest: Canopy, Creatures, and Cryptic Clues - Unlocking the lush labyrinth of life.

IN A REALM WHERE the rainforest reigned supreme, a verdant kingdom of endless green and hidden secrets, there lived a girl named Luna. Luna had a spirit as vibrant as the rainforest canopy and a curiosity as deep as the roots of the ancient trees. She grew up listening to the rainforest symphony, a melody of life, mystery, and untold stories.

Motivated by her love for nature and a desire to understand the secrets of the rainforest, Luna embarked on a journey into its heart. She stepped into the world of green and whispered with a backpack equipped with essentials – a waterproof jacket, a camera, a notepad, and a field guide to the rainforest.

As Luna ventured more profoundly, the rainforest enveloped her in a world unlike any other. The air was a tapestry of bird calls, insect chirps, and the rustling of leaves. The canopy above was a living roof dappled with sunlight, and the ground was carpeted with a mosaic of ferns and flowers.

But the rainforest was more than just beauty; it was a puzzle waiting to be solved. Luna noticed patterns in the way the vines twisted and the trees grew. She saw footprints of creatures unknown, each a clue in this natural labyrinth.

As she delved further, Luna encountered the rainforest's inhabitants. A troop of monkeys swung from the trees, their eyes gleaming with mischief. A brightly colored parrot recited the sounds of the forest, a mimic, and a storyteller. Luna realized each creature was a piece of the puzzle, a part of the rainforest's story.

But the rainforest, in all its splendor, also held challenges. Paths disappeared, rivers changed course, and the dense foliage often seemed like walls of green. Luna used her knowledge and intuition to navigate. She observed the sun's position, the pattern of the leaves, and the flow of the rivers. Her journey was a dance with the forest, each step a note in harmony with nature.

One day, Luna stumbled upon an ancient tree, its trunk as wide as a house. Carved into its bark were symbols and drawings, the legacy of a long past. Fascinated, Luna took out her notepad and began to sketch. She felt like a detective uncovering a secret from an old, forgotten world.

As night fell, the rainforest transformed. The sounds became a chorus of the nocturnal ballet, and the moonlight filtered through the canopy like silver threads. Luna camped under the stars, the forest her guardian and companion.

After days of exploration, Luna emerged from the rainforest, her heart and notepad filled with secrets. She had unraveled some of its mysteries, understanding the language of its paths and the stories of its creatures.

Back in her village, Luna shared her adventure. She spoke of the patterns of life in the rainforest, the importance of each creature and plant, and the delicate balance of this ecosystem:

1. The necessity of observing and learning from nature to understand its intricacies.

2. The importance of respecting and preserving the natural world.

3. The joy of discovery and the value of keeping the mysteries of nature alive.

Luna's journey through the Riddle of the Rainforest became a tale of wonder and wisdom, a testament to the beauty and complexity of this vibrant ecosystem.

# CHAPTER 21

# The Swamp's Hidden Dangers: Mud, Mysteries, and Marshland Maneuvers - Navigating the nifty nuances of the wetlands.

A BOY NAMED ELI lived in a region where the swamp stretched like a vast, mysterious canvas, a place of eerie beauty and hidden perils. Eli had an adventurous heart, as restless as the swamp winds and a curiosity as deep as the murky waters of the marsh.

Driven by tales of lost treasures and ancient secrets hidden in the swamp, Eli embarked on a journey to explore this enigmatic world. With a backpack containing essentials – waterproof boots, a compass, a map, snacks, and a sturdy rope – he ventured into the wetlands, where land and water danced in a delicate balance.

As Eli made his way through the swamp, he was mesmerized by its unique landscape. Towering cypress trees stood like sentinels, their roots sprawling like intricate sculptures. The air was filled with croaking frogs and chirping birds, a symphony of swamp life.

But the swamp was a labyrinth of challenges. The ground was treacherous, a mixture of solid earth and deceptive mud that could swallow a person whole. Eli trod carefully, his steps calculated like those of a chess player. He used his rope to test the firmness of the ground ahead, a lifeline in a world where every step could be a trap.

The dense foliage often seemed impenetrable, and the path was a maze of choices. To navigate, Eli used his compass and map, but he also relied on his instincts and the subtle signs of nature – the direction of the water flow, the position of the sun, and the patterns of the vegetation.

As he delved deeper into the swamp, Eli encountered its inhabitants. A snake slithered away into the underbrush, its presence a reminder of the hidden dangers. A heron stood statuesque by the water, a master of patience. Eli realized that each creature was an expert in survival in this challenging environment.

One of the most captivating moments came when Eli stumbled upon an old, sunken boat, half-buried in the mud. It was as if he had discovered a relic from another era. He imagined the stories the ship could tell, tales of the swamp and those who dared to navigate its waters.

As night approached, the swamp transformed. The sounds became more mysterious and the shadows longer. Eli set up a makeshift camp on a small, dry patch. The night in the swamp was an experience like no other – a mix of awe and apprehension under a canopy of stars barely visible through the tree branches.

Eli continued his exploration the following day, each step taking him deeper into the swamp's heart. He sketched the plants and noted the wildlife, a young naturalist documenting this wild, watery world.

After days of exploration, Eli emerged from the swamp with a new understanding of this unique ecosystem. He had not found any lost treasures, but he had uncovered the secrets of the swamp – its challenges, beauty, and role in the larger environment.

Back in his town, Eli shared his adventure, his stories a blend of excitement and caution:

1. The importance of preparing and respecting the swamp's dangerous yet fascinating environment.

2. The necessity of being aware of one's surroundings and understanding the nuances of navigating such a landscape.

3. The value of preserving these wetlands and learning from their intricate ecosystems.

Eli's journey through the Swamp's Hidden Dangers became a tale of adventure and respect for one of nature's most mysterious landscapes.

# CHAPTER 22

# The Sudden Snowstorm: Blizzards, Bravery, and Icy Intuition - Weathering the whims of a wintry wonderland.

IN A QUAINT TOWN nestled at the foot of snow-capped mountains, where each winter wrapped the landscape in a blanket of white, there lived a girl named Emma. Emma had a spirit as bright as a snowflake and a resilience as strong as the pine trees that stood against the winter winds.

Driven by a love for the snowy peaks and a desire to experience the serene beauty of the mountains in winter, Emma set out on a hiking adventure. She was well-prepared, her backpack equipped with thermal clothing, a flask of hot tea, a compass, a map, and a first-aid kit. She stepped into the winter wonderland with a heart full of excitement and eyes sparkling like the snow under the sun.

As Emma trekked through the snowy landscape, the world around her was a vision of pristine beauty. The snow-laden trees stood in silent majesty, and the crisp air sang with the whispers of winter. Emma felt as if she were walking through the pages of a fairy tale, each step a note in this wintry melody.

But as is often the case in the mountains, the weather had a mind. Without warning, the sky darkened, and what began as a gentle snowfall quickly turned into a roaring snowstorm. A swirling white fury swallowed the world around Emma as if a giant had shaken a massive snow globe.

Emma knew the dangers of being caught in a snowstorm. She remembered the lessons from her mountain safety classes – in a blizzard, shelter and staying warm were crucial. She found a sheltered spot under a sturdy tree and used her backpack as a makeshift windbreak. Pulling her thermal blanket around her, she became a lone island in a sea of swirling snow.

The snowstorm raged around her, a dance of nature's raw power. Emma stayed calm, her mind clear like the ice crystals that formed on her jacket. She knew panic was like the wind in the storm, wild and unhelpful.

As hours passed and the storm continued, Emma relied on her icy intuition. She kept moving her arms and legs to stay warm, sipped her hot tea, and checked her compass and map with the light of her flashlight. She was not just fighting the storm but dancing with it, a dance of survival and wit.

Finally, after what seemed like an eternity, the storm began to wane. The furious winds calmed, and the snowfall slowed to a gentle waltz. Emma emerged from her shelter, a survivor of the mountain's whims.

Her journey back was cautious but steady. Now a fresh canvas of untouched snow, the landscape was both a challenge and a marvel. Emma navigated her way around, her every step a testament to her bravery and resilience.

Emma's tale of the sudden snowstorm became a story of courage and survival upon her return. She shared her experience, emphasizing the lessons she learned:

1. The importance of respecting the unpredictability of mountain weather.

2. The necessity of proper preparation and the value of survival skills in extreme conditions.

3. The power of staying calm and using knowledge and intuition in adversity.

Emma's adventure in the sudden snowstorm was more than a tale of braving the elements; it was a journey of self-discovery and respect for the majestic yet formidable nature of the mountains.

# CHAPTER 23

# The Night in the Northern Lights: Auroras, Adventures, and Arctic Antics - A polar pursuit under the dancing skies.

IN A LAND WHERE the night sky danced with colors, and the cold air sang with the whispers of the Arctic, there lived a boy named Erik. Erik had a heart filled with wanderlust and a mind as sharp as the icicles that adorned his village. The Northern Lights had always fascinated him with their mystical ballet of lights.

One winter evening, driven by a yearning to witness the celestial spectacle up close, Erik embarked on a journey into the Arctic wilderness. He was well-prepared for the Arctic's erratic temperament, his backpack stocked with thermal gear, a sleeping bag, a portable stove, and emergency supplies.

As Erik ventured deeper into the Arctic expanse, the world around him was a canvas of white, the snow sparkling like a sea of diamonds under the moonlight. The air was crisp and fresh, each breath a cloud of swirling mist.

But the Arctic, a land of beauty and peril, soon showed its unpredictable nature. The weather shifted, the winds howling like wolves in the night, and the temperature dropped as if the night had decided to wrap the world in a blanket of frost.

Erik, aware of the challenges of Arctic travel, set up camp in a sheltered area. He carefully pitched his tent, its walls a barrier between him and the icy clutches of the Arctic night. He used his stove to melt snow for water; each sips a treasure in this frozen desert.

As the night deepened, Erik stepped out of his tent, and there it was – the Northern Lights. Ribbons of green and purple danced across the sky, a cosmic show of lights. Erik stood in awe, his eyes wide with wonder, his heart dancing with the lights. It was as if the sky was telling stories, tales of the universe and its many mysteries.

But the beauty of the Northern Lights was not without its dangers. The cold was a silent predator, and Erik knew he had to be vigilant. He kept his body warm, moving around and sipping warm drinks, his actions a dance to the rhythm of survival.

Through the night, Erik marveled at the spectacle above. The Northern Lights were more than just lights; they were a connection to something greater, a bridge between Earth and the cosmos.

As dawn approached, Erik packed up his camp, painting the sky with soft hues of pink and blue. His journey back reflected his experiences, each step a memory of the night's wonders and challenges.

Upon his return, Erik's tale of the Northern Lights became a story of adventure and awe. He shared his experience, emphasizing the lessons he learned:

1. The importance of preparation and respect for the harsh yet beautiful Arctic environment.

2. The necessity of staying vigilant and maintaining warmth in extreme cold.

3. The power of witnessing nature's wonders and the humbling experience of the Northern Lights.

Erik's night under the Northern Lights was more than just a pursuit of beauty; it was a journey of respect and admiration for one of nature's most extraordinary displays.

# CHAPTER 24

# The Sands of the Ancient Ruins: Relics, Riddles, and Resilient Routes - Unearthing secrets and surviving the ancient sands.

THERE LIVED A GIRL named Zara in a land where history whispered from the ancient sands and the sun ruled the sky with a golden scepter. Zara had a spirit as indomitable as the desert winds and a curiosity as vast as the sprawling dunes. She had grown up listening to tales of lost cities and ancient civilizations buried beneath the sands.

One scorching morning, fueled by her thirst for discovery, Zara embarked on a journey to explore the ancient ruins said to be hidden deep within the desert. She was well-prepared for the desert's trials, her backpack equipped with water, a sun hat, a map, a compass, and a journal for her findings.

As Zara ventured into the heart of the desert, the dunes rose around her like waves in a golden sea. The sun beat down relentlessly, a fiery guardian of the desert's secrets. But Zara's resolve was as unyielding as the ancient stones she sought.

The desert was a labyrinth of shifting sands and hidden paths. Zara used her compass and map to navigate, her every step dancing with the desert. She observed the patterns in the sand and the way the dunes were shaped by the wind, using them as guides to lead her to her destination.

After hours of trekking under the blazing sun, Zara stumbled upon something extraordinary – the ruins of an ancient city, its walls half-buried under the sand, standing as a testament to a forgotten era. The sight took her breath away. It was like stepping into another world of shadows and sun-baked stones.

The ruins were a maze of corridors and collapsed chambers. Zara explored with reverence, her heart racing with every discovery – fragments of pottery, ancient inscriptions on the walls, and mysterious symbols that hinted at lost knowledge.

But as Zara delved deeper into the ruins, she realized the dangers of this forgotten city. Walls threatened to crumble, and hidden crevices lurked beneath the sands. She trod carefully, her every step measured, her senses alert to the whispers of the ancient stones.

As the day waned, Zara knew she had to return. The desert was not a place to be caught in after dark. Using her map and the position of the setting sun, she retraced her steps back through the sands, her mind a treasure trove of discoveries.

Zara's tale of the ancient ruins became a story of awe and inspiration in her village. She shared her experiences, emphasizing the lessons she learned:

1. The importance of preparation and respect for the desert's vast and un-forgiving nature.

2. The value of observing and under-standing the environment to navi-gate and uncover its secrets.

3. The thrill of exploration and the re-spect for history and ancient civilizations.

Zara's journey to the Sands of the Ancient Ruins was more than an adventure; it was a journey through time, a testament to her courage and the enduring mysteries of the past.

# CHAPTER 25

# The Enigma of the Ebbing Tide: Shorelines, Shells, and Seaside Sagacity - The tidal tales of the ever-changing shore.

A BOY NAMED NOAH lived in a coastal village where the sea sang lullabies at dusk and the horizon whispered of distant lands. Noah had a fascination for the sea as deep as the ocean and a mind as curious as the creatures that dwelled within its depths. The ebbing and flowing tides, with their rhythmic dance, had always captivated him.

One bright morning, armed with a spirit of exploration and a backpack filled with essentials – a tide chart, a notebook, water, and a camera – Noah set out to unravel the enigma of the ebbing tide. He wanted to understand the secrets that the tide revealed and concealed.

The sea retreated as Noah walked along the shoreline, leaving behind a world usually hidden beneath the waves. The ebbing tide revealed the beach as a treasure trove: a mosaic of shells, seaweed, and intriguing rock pools teeming with marine life.

Noah ventured further, his eyes wide with wonder. Each rock pool was a miniature world, a microcosm of the ocean. He observed starfish clinging to the rocks, crabs scuttling in the shallows, and tiny fish darting through the water. He documented these discoveries with his notebook and camera, a young naturalist in his element.

But the sea, with all its beauty, also held dangers. Noah knew that the tides were as unpredictable as the wind. He kept a vigilant eye on the water and regularly checked his tide chart. Like a sleeping giant, the wave could return swiftly, reclaiming what it had left behind.

As he explored, Noah discovered more than life in the tide pools. He found fragments of pottery and old shipwrecks half-buried in the sand, each a relic telling a story of voyages and adventures from long ago.

But the sea began to stir, the tide turning as the moon pulled the waters back to embrace the shore. Noah, mindful of the time, started his journey back. The beach transformed with the returning tide, the sea again covering its secrets.

Noah's path back was a race against the tide. He maneuvered through the rising waters with the agility of a seagull. His understanding of the tides, gained from hours of study and observation, guided him safely back to the village.

Back home, Noah's adventure became a tale of wonder and wisdom. He shared his experiences, emphasizing the lessons he learned:

1. The importance of understanding and respecting the natural rhythms of the sea.

2. The joy of exploration and the value of observing and knowing from the environment.

3. The necessity of being aware and prepared for the changing tides and the power of the sea.

Noah's exploration of the ebbing tide became a story of discovery and respect for the dynamic and ever-changing world of the shoreline, a testament to the beauty and mystery of the sea.

# CHAPTER 26

# The Festival of Forgotten Friends: Joy, Rekindling, and Childhood Chums - The enchantment of rediscovering old bonds.

I N A SMALL, PICTURESQUE town, wrapped in the warmth of its close-knit community and the charm of its quaint streets, there lived a girl named Ava. Ava had a smile that could light up the darkest room and a heart as open as the sky. She cherished her friendships, each a precious gem in the treasure chest of her memories.

One crisp autumn day, the town announced the Festival of Forgotten Friends, a celebration designed to reunite old friends and rekindle childhood bonds. Ava, thrilled by the idea, decided to embark on a quest to find her childhood friends, with whom she had lost touch over the years.

Equipped with a scrapbook filled with memories, a list of names, and a heart full of hope, Ava set out on her journey. The town, bustling with excitement for the upcoming festival, hums with the melody of reconnection.

Ava's first stop was the old neighborhood park, the site of countless childhood adventures. There, she found her friend Max, once a naughty boy but now a thoughtful artist. They reminisced about their days of play and mischief, their laughter echoing like a song from the past.

Next, Ava visited the local library, a haven of stories and dreams. Among the stacks of books, she rediscovered Lily, a childhood confidante, now a librarian with a love for stories as vast as the ocean. They shared tales of the books they had read and the lives they had led since their last meeting.

As the day progressed, Ava continued her quest. She reconnected with friends at old haunts and favorite spots, each reunion a stitch in the fabric of her childhood. There was Noah, who had once traded baseball cards with her and was now a little league coach; Emily, her partner in dance recitals, was now a ballet instructor; and many others.

Ava's scrapbook grew more prosperous with each friend she found, filled with new memories alongside the old. The laughter, the stories, and the warmth of rekindled friendships enveloped Ava in a new and familiar joy.

The Festival of Forgotten Friends arrived, a carnival of joy and nostalgia. The town square was alive with music, dancing, and reunion sounds. Ava and her friends, old and new, celebrated together, their childhood bonds as strong as ever.

Under the starlit sky, Ava realized the true magic of the festival. It wasn't just about remembering the past but bringing those cherished memories into the present and future. It celebrated friendship, life's journey, and the threads connecting us all.

Back home, Ava's heart was whole. She had embarked on a journey to find her forgotten friends but had found so much more. She shared her story, emphasizing the lessons she learned:

1. The timeless value of friendships and the importance of keeping them alive.

2. The joy of revisiting old memories and creating new ones.

3. The beauty of community and the power of coming together to celebrate shared histories.

Ava's adventure at the Festival of Forgotten Friends became a story of love, laughter, and the enduring magic of friendships, a reminder that some bonds, no matter how old, never indeed fade.

# CHAPTER 27

# The Whirlwind of Wrong Directions: Map Reading, Navigation Skills, and Misadventures - Mastering the maze of streets and signs.

IN A BUSTLING CITY, a maze of streets and alleys, where every turn led to new adventures and the unknown lurked around every corner, there lived a boy named Leo. Leo had an insatiable curiosity for exploration and a knack for getting into and out of trouble. With its labyrinthine layout, the city was his playground and his puzzle.

One sunny afternoon, driven by a desire to master the art of navigation, Leo embarked on a challenge – to traverse the city using only a map and his wits without relying on technology. Armed with a city map, a compass, and a sense of adventure, he embarked on his journey of discovery.

As Leo navigated through the city, he was amazed by its diversity. The streets were like veins, pulsing with life, each neighborhood a different heartbeat. He crossed bustling marketplaces where the air was thick with the aroma of spices, passed quiet parks where the only sound was the rustling of leaves, and wandered through busy squares echoing hundreds' footsteps.

But the city was a tricky teacher. Streets that seemed straightforward on the map twisted and turned unexpectedly. Leo walked in circles, the buildings and signs mocking him like mischievous spirits. He realized that reading a map was more than just following lines; it was about understanding the city's language.

Leo used landmarks as his guides, the tall spire of a church or the unique facade of a museum serving as waypoints in his urban expedition. He began to see the patterns of the streets, the way they flowed and intersected. His compass was his ally, pointing him in the right direction when the city's winding ways tried to confuse him.

Leo's adventure became more challenging as the day turned into an evening. The setting sun changed the city's colors and shadows, making familiar streets into unknown territories. But Leo's confidence in his navigation skills grew. He started to enjoy the challenge; each wrong turn was a lesson, and each right turn was a victory.

Finally, after hours of exploring, deciphering, and occasionally getting lost, Leo found his way back to his starting point. He had traversed the city, navigating its confusing layout and learning its secrets.

Returning home, Leo felt a sense of accomplishment. He tackled the Whirlwind of Wrong Directions and became more knowledgeable and confident. He shared his adventure with friends and family, emphasizing the lessons he learned:

1. The importance of understanding and developing navigation skills in an increasingly digital world.

2. The value of using landmarks and environmental clues for orientation.

3. The joy of exploration and learning comes from making and correcting mistakes.

Leo's adventure through the city's maze became a tale of resilience, resourcefulness, and the timeless art of navigation, a reminder of the importance of knowing how to find one's way in the world.

# CHAPTER 28

# The Secret of the Silent Friend: Whispers, Woes, and Winning Smiles - Learning to listen to unspoken words.

IN A LIVELY NEIGHBORHOOD where laughter echoed through the streets and every house held a story, a girl named Mia lived. Mia smiled like springtime and had a heart as big as the sky. She loved talking to her friends and sharing stories and dreams under the shade of the old oak tree in the park.

One day, Mia noticed something unusual. Her friend, Lucas, who was usually as chatty as a magpie, had become quiet, his usual bright eyes now a little dim. Lucas seemed to have retreated into a shell at school, in the park, and even during their weekend bike rides.

Concerned and puzzled, Mia decided to unravel her silent friend's secret. She knew that sometimes the loudest cries for help were silent, hidden behind a smile or a quiet nod.

She started by spending more time with Lucas, inviting him after school. Mia talked less and listened more, giving Lucas space to open up. She noticed little things - a sigh here, a hesitant glance there, small pieces of a giant puzzle.

One afternoon, as they sat in Mia's backyard, Lucas finally shared his troubles. His parents were going through a tough time, and the confusion and sadness of it all were weighing on him. He had been silent because he didn't want to burden anyone with his problems.

Mia listened, her heart aching for her friend. She didn't offer quick fixes or dismiss his feelings. Instead, she just sat with him, her presence a silent pillar of support. She showed him that he wasn't alone, that his feelings mattered, and that she was there for him, come rain or shine.

In the days that followed, Mia continued to be there for Lucas. She found little ways to brighten his day - a funny note in his locker, a homemade cookie with his lunch, or just a smile across the classroom.

Slowly, Lucas began to find his voice again. His smile and laughter returned like the first sun rays after a long night. He thanked Mia for her silent understanding and unwavering support, for being a friend who listened with her ears and heart.

Mia's journey with Lucas taught her an invaluable lesson - that true friendship isn't just about sharing laughs and good times. It's also about being there in the silence, listening to the unspoken words, and understanding the whispers of a friend's heart.

Back at school, Mia shared her experience with her classmates. Her story became a lesson in empathy and kindness:

1. The importance of being attentive to friends' unspoken emotions and changes in behavior.

2. The value of patience and silent support in helping friends through tough times.

3. The power of empathy in strengthening friendships and building emotional connections.

Mia's story of discovering the secret of her silent friend became a testament to the power of listening, understanding, and the unspoken bonds of friendship.

# CHAPTER 29

# The Puzzle of the Missing Things: Clues, Confusion, and Clever Discoveries - Unraveling the mystery of lost items.

A BOY NAMED OLIVER lived in a vibrant neighborhood where every house was a different color, and every garden bloomed with stories. Oliver had a keen mind, always buzzing with questions, and a knack for solving puzzles. However, Oliver faced a peculiar challenge – things around his house had a way of mysteriously disappearing.

It all started with small things: a sock and a pencil. But soon, more items began to vanish – his favorite comic book, a model airplane he had spent weeks building, even his cherished baseball cap. The house seemed to swallow things whole, leaving Oliver baffled and frustrated.

Determined to solve this mystery, Oliver turned detective. He equipped himself with a notepad and a magnifying glass, ready to hunt for clues. His room became the first scene of the investigation, a landscape of toys, books, and hidden treasures.

As Oliver scoured his room, he found the first clue – a trail of breadcrumbs leading under his bed. Kneeling, flashlight in hand, he discovered a hidden world of lost items. But how did they get there?

Oliver's investigation led him to the next clue – his little sister, Lily. With her mischievous smile and endless curiosity, Lily had been exploring and inadvertently hiding his things in her imaginary games.

Instead of getting upset, Oliver saw an opportunity. He invited Lily to join his detective team, turning the frustration of lost items into a fun game of hide-and-seek. Together, they searched the house, finding each missing item and uncovering the stories behind their disappearance.

Oliver also realized the importance of organization. He began to keep his things in specific places and encouraged Lily to do the same. They created a 'Lost and Found' box for anything they found out of place, turning their detective game into a daily routine.

The mystery of the missing things soon became an adventure for Oliver and Lily. They explored, laughed, and learned together. And as they found each lost item, they also discovered new ways to connect and help each other.

Oliver shared his tale of the missing things at the neighborhood block party. His story became a lesson in problem-solving and patience:

1. The importance of observation and investigation in solving everyday mysteries.

2. The value of turning a challenging situation into a positive, bonding experience.

3. The significance of organization and teamwork in finding solutions.

Oliver's adventure with the puzzle of the missing things taught him not just about finding lost items but also about understanding, cooperation, and the joy of turning problems into fun challenges.

# CHAPTER 30

# The Dilemma of the Broken Widget: Gears, Gizmos, and Great Ideas - Fixing things with innovation and ingenuity.

IN A BUSTLING TOWN known for its inventive spirit and colorful markets, where every street corner boasted a gadget or gizmo, a girl named Clara lived. Clara had a mind like a whirlwind of ideas and hands as skilled as a master tinkerer. She loved separating things, understanding their inner workings, and combining them.

One day, Clara faced a peculiar challenge. The town's beloved clock tower, a marvel of gears and springs, had stopped ticking. The clock, a centerpiece of the town square, symbolized timely order and community pride for as long as anyone could remember.

Clara, driven by her passion for mechanics and a deep sense of community pride, volunteered to repair the clock. She gathered her tools – screwdrivers, wrenches, and an oil can – and determinedly set off for the tower.

As Clara began her work, she realized the task's complexity. The clock was an intricate network of gears, each interlocking with the next in a delicate balance. Years of wear and tear had taken their toll, and several parts needed replacing.

Undeterred, Clara worked meticulously, her hands moving with the precision of a surgeon. She dismantled the clock piece by piece, laying out the gears like a metallic puzzle waiting to be solved. Each component was cleaned, oiled, and examined for wear.

But the real challenge came when Clara discovered a crucial gear was beyond repair. The gear, a unique piece of the clock's mechanism, could be something other than easily replaced. Clara stood before a crossroads of innovation and tradition.

That night, Clara couldn't sleep. Her mind raced with possibilities and designs. Then, in the quiet hours of the morning, an idea struck her like a lightning bolt. She decided to create a new gear that would honor the clock's original design and bring a touch of modern ingenuity.

The next day, with renewed vigor, Clara set to work. She used the town's small workshop to craft the new gear, employing techniques she had learned from her father, a skilled craftsman. The process was challenging and required several attempts, but Clara's persistence shone brighter than the setbacks.

Finally, after days of hard work, Clara fitted the new gear into the clock. With bated breath, she wound the clock and released the pendulum. To her delight and the town's collective relief, the clock began to tick again, its chimes ringing clear and accurate across the square.

Clara's success with the clock tower became the talk of the town. She shared her experience, emphasizing the lessons she learned:

1. The value of understanding and respecting the intricacies of mechanics and heritage.

2. The importance of persistence and creative problem-solving in the face of challenges.

3. The joy of contributing to one's community and the satisfaction of restoring something of collective value.

Clara's journey with the dilemma of the broken widget was more than a tale of repair; it was a story of innovation, respect for tradition, and the triumph of ingenuity.

# CHAPTER 31

# The Unexpected Journey on Public Transport: Tickets, Turns, and Timely Tales - Navigating the network of city transit.

A BOY NAMED MAX lived in a bustling metropolis, a tapestry of streets and lights where every day was a new adventure. Max had an explorer's heart and a zest for life as vibrant as the city. Despite the city's size, Max had always relied on his bike or walks to get around. One day, he decided to tackle a new challenge – navigating the city's public transport network.

Armed with a transit map, a day pass, and a sense of adventure, Max embarked on his journey. He wanted to experience the city from a different perspective, to see its diverse neighborhoods and understand the rhythm of its transit system.

Max's first challenge was the subway. The underground labyrinth was a pulsating web of trains and tunnels. The rush of people, the arriving and departing trains, and the maze of signs were both exhilarating and over-whelming. Max learned to scan the map, identifying the right lines and stops. Each train ride was a lesson in timing and orientation.

Next, Max braved the city buses. He learned the importance of knowing the routes and schedules. Each bus stop was a new scene, with people from all walks of life coming and going. Max enjoyed the sights, peering out the window as the cityscape changed from busy downtown streets to quiet suburban lanes.

But the journey wasn't without its hiccups. Max missed a stop and found himself in an unfamiliar part of the city. Though initially unsettling, the experience turned into an unexpected adventure. He explored the neighborhood, saw a quaint park he never knew existed, and enjoyed local treats from a small bakery.

As the day progressed, Max discovered the unsung beauty of public transport. He observed the city's pulse, the people who moved within it, and the intricate system that connected it all. He initiated conversations with fellow passengers, each sharing snippets of their lives, a mosaic of the city's human tapestry.

By evening, Max had traversed much of the city. He had ridden subways, buses, and even a tram. He had seen parts of the town he'd never visited and learned the value of public transport in connecting lives and places.

Returning home, Max shared his story with friends and family. He spoke of his adventures and the lessons he learned:

1. The importance of understanding and using public transportation as a way to connect with different parts of the city.

2. The value of being open to unexpected detours and discoveries.

3. The joy of seeing the city from a new perspective and the sense of community in shared journeys.

Max's unexpected journey on public transport became a story of discovery and connection, a testament to the city's vibrant life and the threads that weave its people together.

# CHAPTER 32

# Join Our Adventure Squad!

Dear Daring Reader,

Wow, what a journey we've been on together! From scaling the highest peaks to uncovering the mysteries of the deep, you've been there through every twist, turn, and thrilling leap. We hope your heart raced with excitement and your imagination soared to new heights with each story in **"Amazing Adventure and Survival Stories for Young and Curious."**

But the adventure doesn't have to end here! We'd be over the moon (and maybe even around a few mysterious forests and across some uncharted waters) to hear your thoughts about our journey together. Your thoughts, favorite moments, and wildest dreams for new adventures are eagerly awaited!

Please share your review. Whether with friends, family or on your favorite book review site, every word from you is a treasure more precious than the rarest gem in the deepest jungle.

**Here's How You Can Help:**

- **Share Your Thoughts**: What adventures did you love? Which brave characters felt like friends?

- **Spread the Word**: Tell your fellow explorers, friends, and family about our tales. Every new reader is a new friend in our Adventure Squad!

- **Dream Big**: Have an idea for an adventure? We'd love to hear where your imagination takes you!

Your reviews brighten our day and help other young adventurers discover the magic within these pages. Together, we can inspire more curious minds to embark on journeys of discovery and courage.

Thank you for being an essential part of our adventure. Here's to many more!

With heartfelt gratitude and a sprinkle of stardust for your next adventure,

*Magda Lena*

P.S. Keep exploring, keep dreaming, and above all, keep being the fantastic adventurer that you are!

https://www.amazon.com/author/mark.k.j

CAVE of ECHOES

COCONUTS
AND
CASTAWAYS

VINES & VENOM

SNOW AND STARS

PEAKS & PATHS

FLASH FLOOD
RIVERS & RAINS

QUAKE

SWAMP

VOLCANO'S
— SECRET —

SNOW SECCRETS
SURVIVAL SIGNALS

THE STORM